D1366180

JET   2013

WITHDRAWN

DAY BY DAY WITH...

MIA HAMM

BY
TAMMY GAGNE

PUBLISHERS

P.O. Box 196
Hockessin, Delaware 19707
Visit us on the web: www.mitchelllane.com
Comments? Email us:
mitchelllane@mitchelllane.com

Copyright © 2013 by Mitchell Lane Publishers. All rights reserved. No part of this book may be reproduced without written permission from the publisher. Printed and bound in the United States of America.

Printing   1   2   3   4   5   6   7   8   9

RANDY'S CORNER

DAY BY DAY WITH. . .

Beyoncé	Mia Hamm
Bindi Sue Irwin	Miley Cyrus
Chloë Moretz	Selena Gomez
Dwayne "The Rock" Johnson	Shaun White
Eli Manning	Steve Hillenburg
Justin Bieber	Taylor Swift
LeBron James	Willow Smith

Library of Congress Cataloging-in-Publication Data
Gagne, Tammy.
 Day by day with Mia Hamm / by Tammy Gagne.
    p. cm. — (Randy's corner)
 Includes bibliographical references and index.
 ISBN 978-1-61228-327-2 (library bound)
 1. Hamm, Mia, 1972– —Juvenile literature. 2. Soccer players—United States—Biography—Juvenile literature. 3. Women soccer players—United States—Biography—Juvenile literature. I. Title.
 GV942.7.H27G34 2013
 796.334092—dc23
 [B]
                                                  2012018312

eBook ISBN: 9781612283968

ABOUT THE AUTHOR: Tammy Gagne has written dozens of books for children, including *Day by Day with Justin Bieber* and *What It's Like to Be Cameron Diaz*. One of her favorite pastimes is visiting schools to speak to kids about the writing process.

PUBLISHER'S NOTE: The following story has been thoroughly researched and to the best of our knowledge represents a true story. While every possible effort has been made to ensure accuracy, the publisher will not assume liability for damages caused by inaccuracies in the data and makes no warranty on the accuracy of the information contained herein. This story has not been authorized or endorsed by Mia Hamm.

PLB

DAY BY DAY WITH

MIA HAMM

4

Mia Hamm is one of the most famous athletes in the world today. No soccer player in history—either male or female—has scored as many international goals as Mia has.

On March 17, 1972, Bill and Stephanie Hamm had their fourth child. They named her Mariel Margaret Hamm—"Mia" for short. Stephanie was a former ballet dancer, and she had a teacher by the name of Mia Slavenska whom she admired greatly. This is where the Hamms got Mia's nickname.

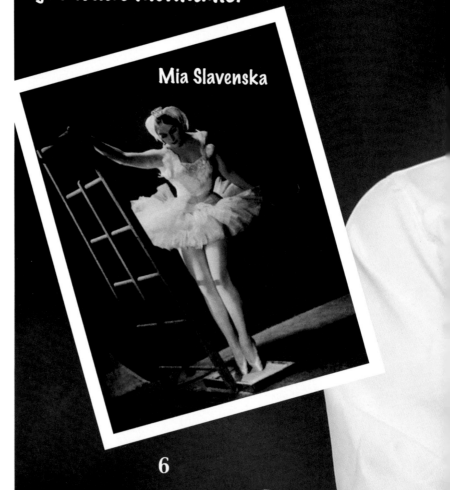

Mia Slavenska

Born with a partial clubfoot, Mia had to wear casts on her feet as an infant so she could walk like other children when she got older. Mia's sister Caroline shares with CNN, "As soon as those things were taken off her feet, you could not stop her." Still, no one could have guessed that Mia would grow up to become a professional soccer player.

Normal
baby foot

Clubfoot
of a baby

Mia was born in Selma, Alabama, but she didn't stay there for long. Her father was in the Air Force, which meant the family had to move around a lot. In addition to Alabama, Mia lived in California, Texas, Virginia, and even Italy as a child.

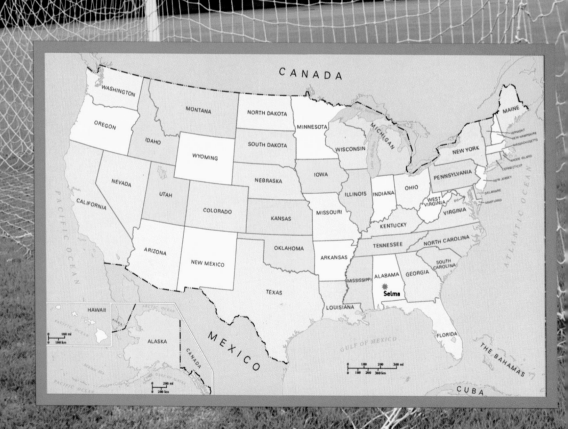

It was in Italy that Mia first discovered soccer. Caroline tells CNN, "Mia was in a park in Italy playing, and the next thing they knew, she went darting across the green. And she was taking away a soccer ball from a kid that was five years old, and she was maybe two."

MIA

MIA (RIGHT) CHALLENGES LAURA JONES FOR THE BALL AT THE U.S. OLYMPIC FESTIVAL IN 1989.

When Mia was a little girl, her parents signed her up for ballet. After a couple of lessons, though, she knew she didn't want to be a ballerina. She wanted to play sports instead. When she lived in Texas, Mia played baseball, basketball, tennis, and soccer. She even played football on the boys' middle school team.

MIA (LEFT) GETS READY TO SCORE A GOAL.

By the time Mia entered high school, she had become a dedicated soccer player. Scouts from colleges all over the country came to watch her play. In 1987, she was given the chance to play in an Olympic development tournament. She scored five goals, more than any other player in the tournament. At 15, she became the youngest player in history to earn a spot on the U.S. women's national soccer team.

In 1989, Mia became a student at the University of North Carolina (UNC). In her four years there, she helped the UNC women's soccer team win four NCAA Championships. The year after she graduated, the school retired Mia's number 19 jersey.

FANS

During her college years, Mia brought many new American fans to the sport of soccer. In 1991, she helped the United States win its first-ever Women's World Cup. Her soccer accomplishments would not end there, though.

FANS

WORLD CUP
TROPHY

Mia went on to play in the 1996 Olympics in Atlanta, Georgia. While there, she helped the U.S. women's national soccer team win the gold medal. Three years later, Mia scored her 108th goal. This accomplishment made her the top scorer among both men and women throughout the world.

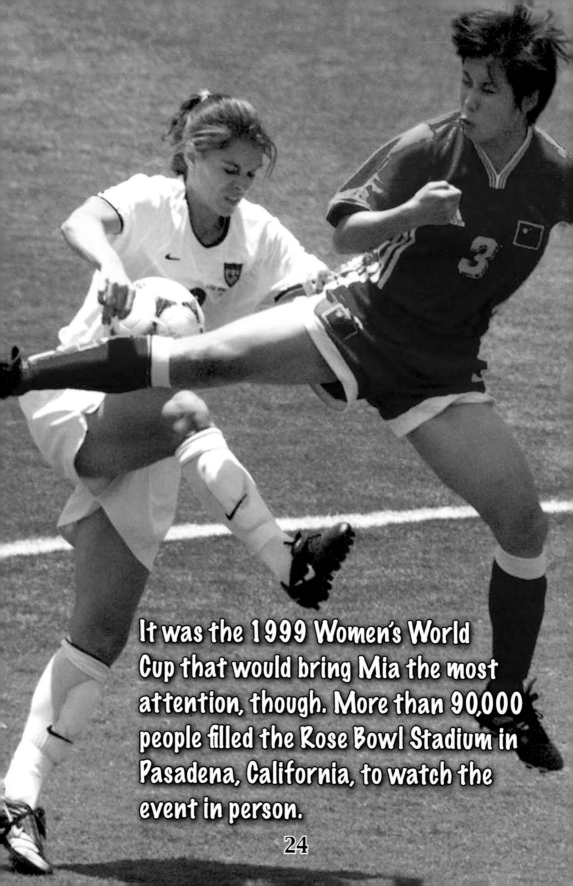

It was the 1999 Women's World Cup that would bring Mia the most attention, though. More than 90,000 people filled the Rose Bowl Stadium in Pasadena, California, to watch the event in person.

Millions of others around the world
watched live on television. In the end, the
United States beat China 5 to 4, making
Mia Hamm a household name.

Mia retired from playing professional soccer in 2004 with a total of 158 international goals and two Olympic gold medals. She then established the Mia Hamm Foundation, an organization that helps raise money to find a cure for bone marrow diseases.

MIA'S FAMILY AND FRIENDS

Mia's older brother, Garrett, died of a rare blood disorder in 1997. The two were very close. "I learned so much through him," Mia told CNN, "about perseverance, about grace, about dignity."

MIA AND HER HUSBAND NOMAR ATTEND A BONE MARROW DRIVE WITH EIGHT-YEAR-OLD ANTHONY ARROYO. ANTHONY ONCE RECEIVED A BONE MARROW TRANSPLANT HIMSELF.

Today Mia is married to professional baseball player Nomar Garciaparra. The two have twin daughters, Ava and Grace, who were born in 2007. But Mia still finds time for soccer, and volunteers to teach children about the game she loves so much.

AS THE SPOKESPERSON FOR DANNON'S LIVE YOUR ACTIVE CULTURE PROGRAM, MIA TEACHES FAMILIES ABOUT HEALTH AND WELLNESS THROUGH SOCCER CLINICS LIKE THIS ONE.

Mia says that she and Nomar will not push their girls to be soccer or baseball players. "They're their own people," she points out to *Redbook*. "One of my daughters wants to take ballet, and I'd love that." But if either Ava or Grace does decide to play soccer, they couldn't ask for a better soccer mom.

FURTHER READING

BOOKS

Hamm, Mia. *Winners Never Quit!* New York: HarperCollins, 2004.

Zarzycki, Daryl Davis. *Mia Hamm.* Hockessin, DE: Mitchell Lane Publishers, 2005.

ON THE INTERNET

KidzWorld: Mia Hamm Biography
http://www.kidzworld.com/article/4656-mia-hamm-biography

Soccer Times: Mia Hamm
http://www.soccertimes.com/usteams/roster/women/hamm.htm

WORKS CONSULTED

Biography.com. "Mia Hamm." http://www.biography.com/people/mia-hamm-16472547

CNN. "Soccer Star Raising Goals in Women's Sports." http://www.cnn.com/CNN/Programs/people/shows/hamm/profile.html

Loveday, Veronica. "Mia Hamm." *Great Athletes of Our Time*, 2011.

Palmer, Lindsey. "Mia Hamm Does 'Soccer Mom' Her Way." *Redbook*, November 2010.

Smith, Gary. "The Secret Life of Mia Hamm." *Sports Illustrated*, September 17, 2003.

INDEX

PHOTO CREDITS: Cover—Jed Jacobsohn/Getty Images; pp. 4–5—AP Photo/PRNewsFoto/The Dannon Company; p. 5—AP Photo/Armando Franca; pp. 6–7—Lisa Blumenfield/Getty Images; p. 8—Sports Illustrated for Kids; p. 9—Jeff Gross/Allsport/Getty Images; p. 11—Rick Stewart/Allsport/Getty Images; pp. 12, 13, 14—Getty Images; p. 15—AP Photo/Angela Rowlings; pp. 16–17—John R. Van Beekum/The Washington Post via Getty Images; p. 18—Will McIntyre/Time Life Pictures/Getty Images; p. 19—Bob Donman/Sports Illustrated/Getty Images; pp. 20–21, 26—Harry How/Getty Images; pp. 22–23—Ezra Shaw/Getty Images; p. 23—AP Photo/Kevork Djansezian; p. 24–25—Hector Mata/AFP/Getty Images; p. 25—Grant Halverson/Allsport/Getty Images; p. 27—AP Photo/Branimir Kvartuc; p. 28—Jon Shohoo/WireImage/Getty Images; pp. 28–29—Casey Rogers/AP Images for Dannon; pp. 30–31—Robert Laberge/Getty Images. Every effort has been made to locate all copyright holders of materials used in this book. Any errors or omissions will be corrected in future editions of the book.